Jobs in Our Community

Veterinarians on the Job

By Anne Forest

KidHaven Publishing

Published in 2017 by
KidHaven Publishing, an Imprint of Greenhaven Publishing, LLC
353 3rd Avenue
Suite 255
New York, NY 10010

Designer: Deanna Paternostro
Editor: Katie Kawa

Photo credits: Cover Wavebreakmedia Ltd/Thinkstock; p. 5 Volt Collection/Shutterstock.com; p. 7 Comstock/Stockbyte/Thinkstock; p. 9 Byelikova Oksana/Shutterstock.com; p. 11 Jevtic/iStock/Thinkstock; p. 13 ullstein bild/Getty Images; p. 15 Olena Yakobchuk/Shutterstock.com; p. 17 Anan Kaewkhammul/Shutterstock.com; p. 19 VGstockstudio/Shutterstock.com; p. 21 didesign021/iStock/Thinkstock; p. 23 fotoedu/iStock/Thinkstock.

Library of Congress Cataloging-in-Publication Data

Names: Forest, Anne, author.
Title: Veterinarians on the job / Anne Forest.
Description: New York : KidHaven Publishing, [2017] | Series: Jobs in our community | Includes index.
Identifiers: LCCN 2016036207 (print) | LCCN 2016044078 (ebook) | ISBN 9781534521490 (pbk.) | ISBN 9781534521506 (6 pack) | ISBN 9781534521513 (library bound) | ISBN 9781534521520 (E-book)
Subjects: LCSH: Veterinarians–Juvenile literature. | Veterinary medicine–Juvenile literature.
Classification: LCC SF756 .F67 2017 (print) | LCC SF756 (ebook) | DDC 636.089092–dc23
LC record available at https://lccn.loc.gov/2016036207

Printed in the United States of America

CPSIA compliance information: Batch #CW17KL: For further information contact Greenhaven Publishing LLC, New York, New York at 1-844-317-7404.

Please visit our website, www.greenhavenpublishing.com. For a free color catalog of all our high-quality books, call toll free 1-844-317-7404 or fax 1-844-317-7405.

CONTENTS

Veterinarians help animals stay healthy. They are doctors for animals.

Veterinarians help animals when they are sick or hurt.

Some veterinarians only care for pets such as cats and dogs.

Other veterinarians work with farm animals such as horses and cows.

Zoos have veterinarians, too. They care for the animals that live there.

Veterinarians see how much animals weigh. They use a **scale**.

Animals need shots
to stay healthy.
Veterinarians give
them shots.

A veterinarian checks an animal's eyes, ears, and teeth.

A veterinarian puts a **bandage** on an animal that is hurt. They do this very carefully.

Veterinarians love animals!

WORDS TO KNOW

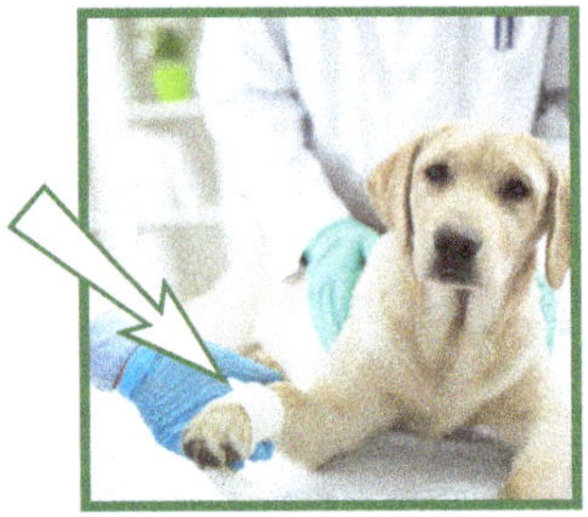

bandage

scale

INDEX